Original title:
Olive Branch Odes

Copyright © 2025 Creative Arts Management OÜ
All rights reserved.

Author: Cameron Blair
ISBN HARDBACK: 978-1-80566-783-4
ISBN PAPERBACK: 978-1-80566-803-9

The Witty Leafy Gesture

In the garden where the greens play,
A spry little tree had nothing to say.
Its twigs danced wildly, then paused for a laugh,
As squirrels debated on which one to cut in half.

The neighbors peered over, in robes quite a sight,
With gossip that fluttered like birds in mid-flight.
"Should we strike some peace, or just poke some fun?"
A fruit bat swooped and declared, "Why not both, hon?"

Chickens clucked wisdom that made no sense,
Discussing the merits of pickle juice hence.
One rooster crowed proudly, "I hold the best card!"
But tripped on a branch, and fell down in the yard.

So here's to that tree, with its quirky embrace,
Creating a haven for all in the space.
If laughter's the aim, then all should partake,
Branch out in delight or just shake it to shake!

Tides of Compassion

When the seas of kindness swell,
Waves of laughter start to yell.
A fish wearing socks swims by,
And tickles the clouds in the sky.

Seagulls laugh with a silly squawk,
As they strut and dance on the dock.
Bigger waves can't spoil the fun,
They just add to the giggles begun.

The Calm After the Storm

After thunder makes its racket,
Rainbows rise in a jeans jacket.
Lightning bugs give a cheerful cheer,
As puddles echo laughter near.

The clouds wear silly grins anew,
While breezes gossip, strong and true.
Nature breathes a comic sigh,
As umbrellas dance and fly.

Harmony's Embrace

In a garden thick with pranks,
Flowers play in silly ranks.
Bumblebees wear tiny hats,
As they waltz with friendly cats.

Mice play tunes on old tin cans,
While rabbits sketch out secret plans.
Harmony hums a joyful song,
Even when things go hilariously wrong.

Serendipitous Encounters

Two socks found on a sunny day,
Set off on an odd ballet.
They twirl beneath the azure sky,
As clouds chant 'Oh my, oh my!'

A hat decides to join the jig,
And starts a dance that's wild and big.
Each step a laugh, a joyous spree,
In the capers of silly glee.

Fruits of Forgiveness

In a garden where we bicker,
Lemons roll with glee, just quicker.
Peaches giggle, cherries chime,
Bananas slip—oh, what a crime!

Tomatoes blush from all the fuss,
While cucumbers just shrug—no muss!
A fruit parade, we're on a spree,
Forgiving bounded by a spree.

Underneath the Canopy of Hope

Underneath the leafy spread,
Snappy squirrels play tag, widespread.
A cat lies dreaming, full of glee,
Of world peace 'neath the apple tree.

The birds are chirping, making plans,
While ants unite with happy fans.
The breeze hums soft, a joke or two,
Hope sprouts high where dreams break through.

The Gentle Gesture of Renewal

One handshake turns into a dance,
As awkward as a grilled cheese romance.
We laugh at all the past mistakes,
And share a pie made of sweet flakes.

The dough's so soft, we can't resist,
Baking memories, none are missed.
A pinch of salt, a dash of zest,
Renewal's recipe, it's the best!

Sowing Seeds of Amity

With seeds of kindness, spread them wide,
The flowers bloom, there's joy inside.
We plant some jokes, outgrow the frowns,
And watch as laughter wears the crowns.

We water with smiles, sunshine bright,
Growing friendships, what a sight!
In this garden, we all agree,
Amity blossoms, wild and free.

Waters of Understanding

In a puddle of thought, I dip my toes,
Where laughter erupts, and wisdom flows.
A splash of wit as we dive right in,
Let's swim through the joys, and toss out the sin.

Fish with glasses swim past on a whim,
They chat about the moonlit gym.
We build a raft of jokes and glee,
Floating in waters of trust, just you and me.

The Gift of Stillness

In a quiet room, the clock goes tick,
A snail in the corner does a little flick.
We pause and ponder with a grin so wide,
Who needs a rush when you can just slide?

The cat on the couch gives me an eye,
As if to say, 'Why rush? Just fly!'
In stillness, we find the giggles tucked tight,
A gift of serenity, wrapped up in light.

Hands Held High

Raise your hands as high as the sky,
Like a bird that forgot how to fly.
We'll wave to the clouds, say hello to the sun,
And make funny faces until we're all done.

In a dance-off with the breeze, we'll sway,
Our hands held high, come what may.
With fingers wiggling and toes in sync,
Let's laugh at the absurd until we all stink!

Spheres of Compassion

In circles we gather, like peas in a pod,
With hearts so big, they're slightly odd.
We toss around kindness like confetti in air,
Each laugh a balloon that floats everywhere.

Our spheres of compassion roll down the street,
Bouncing and laughing, oh what a feat!
We share our giggles and stories so bright,
Creating a tapestry of pure delight.

Blossoms of Forgiveness

A flower bloomed in my best friend's hair,
I laughed so hard, I lost my chair.
We tossed our grudges out the door,
Now we're best pals, can't ask for more!

With petals flung like frisbees high,
We joked and danced as time flew by.
Mistakes were made, but who keeps score?
Who knew forgiveness could be such a roar?

The Soft Embrace of Kindness

A hug so warm, it turned to goo,
We giggled like kids in a zoo.
Forgive my pranks, my silly tricks,
Kindness is like a box of picks.

Tickle, poke, and share a laugh,
Life's too short for a stern photograph.
With kindness wrapped in bubble wrap,
Who knew being nice could be such a slap!

Peaceful Petals in the Wind

Petals drifted while we debated,
Who snored the loudest? Who was elated?
We twirled around those leafy foes,
Every blossom held a secret, who knows?

In gusts of laughter, we spun and whirled,
With heart-shaped leaves, our joy unfurled.
In gentle breezes, we planted seeds,
Of silly stories and outrageous deeds.

An Offering of Hope

I offered a joke, you offered a sigh,
"Did you hear about the fruit that got shy?"
With puns like these, how could we frown?
Turned our frowns completely upside down!

In the garden of laughter, we planted our dreams,
With watered-down humor, or so it seems.
A hope so bright, it caught the sun,
In this merry patch, we all have fun!

Radiant Affection

In a garden where laughter blooms,
Even the gnomes wear silly costumes.
Sunshine giggles, plants twist and sway,
Radiant smiles brighten the day.

Birds wear glasses, perched on a tree,
Chirping jokes as funny as can be.
Squirrels crack jokes, a stand-up show,
Under the sun, their laughter will flow.

Gentle Promises

A cat on a roof plays peek-a-boo,
While a dog dances, doing the woo-hoo.
Clouds drift by, wearing fluffy hats,
As we whisper secrets to the bats.

Promises soft as freshly baked bread,
Mixing giggles with dreams in our head.
A tickle fight under the stars at night,
In this gentle world, everything feels right.

A Haven of Understanding

In a world where socks are always mismatched,
And every fish seems quite attached.
A cozy nook where whispers are sweet,
And the laughter always skips a beat.

Friends like pie, in flavors so wild,
Each a giggly, goofy little child.
Bubbles float high, chasing the breeze,
In this haven, there's never unease.

The Art of Mend

Patchwork hearts stitched with tales untold,
Every seam a hug, a treasure of gold.
We dance to mishaps, wear them with pride,
The art of mend is a joyful ride.

When laughter spills like a cup in a storm,
We gather the spills, creating new form.
In the chaos, we find the delight,
As we stitch together the silly and bright.

The Language of Truce

In a garden where arguments sprout,
We dig for peace down the berry route.
A handshake brought in by the dancing ants,
Where words of war make rude chants.

With giggles and grins, we toss words like balls,
Like squirrels on bicycles racing down halls.
A peace treaty served with a side of cheese,
Laughter floats in the warm summer breeze.

Lullabies of Reconciliation

Whispers of calm hummed to the moon,
Telling off arguments like a big buffoon.
Shushing the noise with a blanket of glee,
Untangling disputes as sweet as can be.

Rock-a-bye battles in the old tree swing,
As melodies banish all fuss and sting.
Snoring through quarrels, we dream of good rhymes,
Till laughter wakes us in silly, fun times.

Beneath the Canopy of Harmony

Under the branches where shadows play,
Frogs croak their peace in a humorous way.
A playful breeze tickles our frowns,
Painting joy where there once were crowns.

Squirrels debate over acorn shares,
Yet they giggle while flipping their fluffy hairs.
With music of chirps and chuckles anew,
We celebrate all that friends can construe.

Blooming Benevolence

Flowers argue, 'Who's the fairest of all?'
While dandelions giggle and twirl with a call.
Petals so bright have a fashion showdown,
Yet peace blooms brightly, wearing a crown.

With bees buzzing humorously 'round the weeds,
They sprinkle good vibes like sweet candy seeds.
In gardens of laughter where all things are fair,
Benevolent blooms dance without a care.

Tunes of Tranquility

In the garden where giggles bloom,
Gnomes dance lightly, to lift the gloom.
A squirrel sings a silly song,
While butterflies join, where they belong.

Petunias nod with a bounce and sway,
While bees wear hats, it's a fancy display.
A breeze whispers jokes through the trees,
And laughter spreads like honeyed teas.

A Call for Harmony

A clumsy cat taps a gentle beat,
As rabbits hop near, they can't find their seat.
The parrot squawks in a tuneful jest,
Who knew friendship could be this blessed?

Amidst the shouts of playful cheer,
Frogs croak ballads for all to hear.
Each note a chuckle, each chord a grin,
Together they're sure to always win.

The Meadow of Togetherness

In a meadow where daisies wear shoes,
Mice serve tea while the critters amuse.
A badger in glasses reads tales of old,
While hedgehogs dance, so brave and bold.

Laughter bubbles like a spring in bloom,
Where every flower is the best kind of room.
They tell tales of pranks and silly dreams,
Amidst the sunlight's warm, golden beams.

Sparks of Rebirth

A turtle flips pancakes, no need for a spatula,
While flamingos break dance, not one bit of failure.
Rabbits juggle carrots like pros on a stage,
As hedgehogs applaud and scream with rage.

With fireworks popping in colors so bright,
Chickens get dizzy but take on the flight.
In a swirl of giggles and twirls of cheer,
The sparkles of friendship always draw near.

A Thoughtful Offering of Harmony

In a world full of chatter,
A gesture can make it all better.
Let's share a snack, not a fight,
With pickles and chips, it feels right.

A peace treaty made in pie,
I promise not to throw a fry.
Together we'll laugh and make noise,
Like kids again, with our toys.

Nurtured Connections in Nature

Underneath the shady trees,
We'll sip our juice and feel the breeze.
Let's braid some grass in silly style,
And dance like we're kids for a while.

The flowers giggle, bees buzz near,
A clumsy bee lands with a cheer.
We'll share our snacks, perhaps a laugh,
Nature's glee is the best path.

The Soft Embrace of Green Vows

A pact made over muddy shoes,
Let's promise to never sing the blues.
With chocolate smeared upon our face,
We'll race each other in this place.

In the garden, we'll plant our dreams,
With funny hats and silly schemes.
Let's paint our joy in colors bright,
Then giggle till dawn turns to light.

Heralds of Truce Beneath the Sky

When clouds above look rather gray,
Let's channel our inner child at play.
A funny hat and playful grin,
Old rivalries tossed in the bin.

With snacks that crumble and a toast,
To friendships that we cherish most.
We'll sing out loud, no need for fear,
While squirrels chuckle, lend an ear.

Echoes of Serenity

In a garden where the gnomes play,
Whispers of peace float by each day.
A squirrel wearing socks glances at me,
Saying, 'Calm down, it's just a cup of tea.'

The birds gossip about last night's feast,
With crumbs of humor, they never cease.
A frog in a hat croaks a joke so sly,
Even the lilies laugh, oh my, oh my!

The Gift of Repose

A cat naps in the sun's warm glow,
Dreaming of fish that dance in a row.
While ants march by with a tiny parade,
The cat twitches, thinking, 'I'm underpaid!'

A tortoise with shades sips lemonade,
Says, 'Slow and steady is how I've laid.'
His friends chuckle as they race around,
But he just smiles, knowing he's profound.

A Swaying Gesture of Unity

The wind plays tricks with the tall grass,
Like a wave of giggles, it dances with sass.
Each blade shouts 'Boo!' at the passing cloud,
While the sun just grins, feeling quite proud.

Two rabbits argue about the best patch,
One says, 'Carrots!' while the other's a match.
They end up laughing until they can't breathe,
A veggie debate, who'd have thought to believe?

Threads of Amity

A spider spins webs with a silly flair,
Each thread whispers secrets that float in the air.
A butterfly joins it, trying to dance,
But trips on a leaf, oh what a chance!

The fireflies laugh at the clumsy show,
Lighting up giggles that softly glow.
As the night hums a funny little tune,
Even the stars wink, under the moon.

Spirit of Calming Boughs

In the garden, squirrels dance,
With acorns tossed, they take a chance.
A crow critiques with cawing glee,
As bees buzz by, oh what a spree!

The sun beams down, a golden ray,
While ants march forth, no time to play.
A little breeze gives trees a laugh,
Nature's show, a comical graph!

The Promise of New Growth

Sprouts peek out, oh what a sight,
A cabbage wore a coat, quite bright.
Gnomes argue who's the sculptor good,
While daisies giggle, knock on wood.

The soil stirs, a worm feels spry,
With wriggly moves, it says goodbye.
Each leafy sprout begins to tease,
With whispers soft in playful breeze.

Whispers of Peace

In the breeze, the willows sway,
Chirping birdcalls join the play.
A garden of laughs blooms so free,
As daisies chuckle at the bee.

The frogs croak out a funny tune,
While crickets join, quite the festoon.
With gentle sighs, the daisies nod,
In nature's waltz, peace is a prod!

Serene Offerings

The pumpkin grins from its patchy throne,
While mushrooms giggle, skin like bone.
A scarecrow chuckles, arms spread wide,
As pumpkins whisper, "Let's go for a ride!"

Underneath, the roots conspire,
Tickling the soil, dreams they acquire.
Serenading night, the crickets play,
Nature's comedy, come what may!

Whispers of Peace Beneath the Boughs

Under the tree, a squirrel forgot,
His stash of nuts in a coffee pot.
The birds all giggle, they can't believe,
Their friend the squirrel must be naive.

A cat strolls by, thinking he's sly,
But he's all whiskers and no reason why.
The peace of the grove, an ironic jest,
Where chaos and calm just love a fest.

A Tapestry of Tranquility

The garden gnome wears shades too bright,
He's sipping tea with the daylight.
A raccoon feasts on leftover fries,
While daisies gossip, oh what a surprise!

The wind starts dancing with a hat on its head,
While butterflies giggle, playing thread.
Amidst this chaos, a nap sounds good,
When the world's so silly, it should!

Harmony's Silent Offering

A bee buzzes loudly, thinks he's a star,
While the ants march on, 'Hey, where's our car?'
The flowers yawn, stretching in the sun,
Making a scene that's just plain fun.

Old man owl hoots, in a drowsy tone,
Telling lame jokes he's fashioned from bone.
But in this grove of giggles and glee,
All creatures laugh, oh yes, even the tree!

The Leaf That Soothes the Soul

One leaf fell down, like a dramatic show,
The crowd erupted, "Bravo! Bravo!"
The breeze gave a bow, with a gusty flair,
As squirrels traded costumes in mid-air.

A turtle tripped, on a passing snail,
Both fell down, without a fail.
Yet in their tumble, joy reigned supreme,
For laughter rippled like a wild dream.

Green Emblems of Concord

In a garden where the goodies grow,
We feast on salad, to and fro.
Lettuce whispers silly jokes,
While carrots giggle, oh what folks!

Beneath the sun, the chives align,
Dancing shadows, sipping brine.
Radishes wearing tiny caps,
Stumble and trip, oh what mishaps!

Gherkins tell tales of fishy dreams,
While broccoli bursts at the seams.
In this patch, where humor sprouts,
Laughter lingers, that's what it's about!

Hold on tight, we're in for a ride,
Veggies grinning from side to side.
With each chuckle, peace will rise,
In this garden, joy never lies.

In the Shade of Reconciliation

Beneath the tree, where whispers play,
Squirrels gossip about the day.
Acorns chuckle in the breeze,
As the sun brings warmth with ease.

Two ants squabble, then hug tight,
Making up by the end of night.
The branches sway, they share a grin,
For laughter is where peace begins!

A frog hops by, croaks a tune,
Under the watchful eye of the moon.
Each croak a jest, each leap a laugh,
In this shade, we find our path.

Even the wind joins in the fun,
Tickling leaves, everyone's on the run.
In this spot, where hearts unwind,
Reconciliation is so kind.

Fertile Hues of Serenity

In a meadow where colors clash,
Sunflowers giggle with a splash.
Daisies dance in polka dots,
While tulips trade the silliest thoughts.

Bees buzzing round with tipsy glee,
Plotting how to sip their tea.
Buttercups clash in yellow fights,
Painting the day with silly sights.

The grass whispers tales of delight,
As daisies twirl in pure sunlight.
In this land of serene cheer,
Laughter blossoms, bringing near.

With every bloom, a chuckle grows,
In this vibrant patch, joy overflows.
Join the dance, don't be late,
For humor is the best of fate!

Echoes of Unity's Embrace

In a hall of mirrors, faces blend,
Reflections giggle, never end.
Each twist and turn a funny scene,
Laughter echoing, crisp and keen.

Unity's song in harmony's tone,
Makes clowns of us, never alone.
With a wink and a nudge, we unite,
And create smiles from morning to night.

Tickling fancies, in tangled strands,
Friends forever, hand in hand.
Jesters rule in this realm bright,
Spreading cheer with sheer delight.

So let's embrace the silly feat,
Together we stand, never to cheat.
In the echoes of laughter's race,
Unity finds its warmest place.

Hearthstones of Connection

In the kitchen, pots collide,
A dinner dance, we won't hide.
Spaghetti flies, a noodle fight,
Laughter shared, on this night.

With burnt toast, we cheer and joke,
Our recipe's a silly cloak.
Coffee spills in joyous glee,
What a mess, just wait and see!

Friends gather 'round with glasses raised,
The toast is warm, our hearts ablaze.
In this kitchen, chaos reigns,
Yet love is found in all the stains.

So here's to moments, silly and bright,
Where every meal becomes delight.
With hearthstones warm, our bonds align,
In laughter's glow, we dine and shine.

An Arc of Trust

Two friends debate, who's right or wrong,
One's always right, or so they're strong.
In a duel of words, they exchange their blows,
With trust between, as friendship grows.

A secret pact, with whispers sly,
Who stole the last slice? Oh my, oh my!
Pinky promises, sworn with a grin,
Their laughter echoes, they both win.

Overboard with jokes, like ships that sail,
In the storm of whimsy, they'll never bail.
An arc so grand, it spans the room,
In the garden of trust, there's always bloom!

Thick and thin, through thickening talk,
With skinned knees, they walk the walk.
With arms outstretched, and trust pure,
In jest and joy, their hearts endure.

The Palette of Peace

Colors splatter, laughter loud,
Painting joy, makes us proud.
With every stroke, a comic tale,
Under our brush, no room to bail.

Splatters here, a dribble there,
Amid the chaos, alright, who cares?
We mix green with a touch of blue,
Creating artwork, silly and true.

While canvases capture the fun and cheer,
Our greatest work? A friendship fierce!
With colors bright, we mingle and mix,
In laughter's hue, our souls we fix.

So let's paint strokes and whirls galore,
With dips and dots, we'll always explore.
In this palette of peppy delight,
Each brush becomes our truth, our light!

In the Shadow of Unity

In shadows deep, our quirks intertwined,
We dance like shadows, two of a kind.
With silly jokes that cause a stir,
Echoes of laughter gently refer.

Under the stars, we share our dreams,
Pantries stocked with sugary creams.
The crumbs of joy around us spread,
In this shadow, hand in hand, we tread.

With mismatched socks and messy hair,
A duo epic, without a care.
We build our fortress made of fun,
Where every moment's a little pun.

So here we thrive, in unity's cheer,
In shadows cast, our bond is clear.
With laughter loud, as light takes flight,
Together we dance into the night.

Songs of Togetherness

Together we dance in mismatched shoes,
Step on toes, sing the wrong blues.
Laughter erupts like popcorn at night,
In our silly chaos, everything feels right.

With legs all tangled, we sway and spin,
Forget the world, let the fun begin.
High-fives turn to fumbles, but who really cares?
In our joyful mess, we're caught unawares.

A chorus of giggles, a melody plays,
We make our own music in the quirkiest ways.
So grab a friend and take a leap,
In the joy of togetherness, our hearts are deep.

From silly songs to ice cream spills,
We cherish each moment, oh what a thrill!
In the dance of life, we find our beat,
Together forever, nothing can compete.

Embracing the Past

We look back at blunders with a chuckle or two,
Remember that time we burnt dinner for fuel?
Family gatherings filled with awkward smiles,
Stories replayed, while time flies for miles.

Digging through boxes, we find the old toys,
Those questionable fashions, and high-pitched noise.
Laughter erupts as we play dress-up again,
With mismatched outfits, we're the best of friends.

While memories fade like a crayon in sun,
We hold onto joy, every laugh that we've spun.
With every mishap, we build and embrace,
A past overflowing with silly grace.

Through thick and thin, we find our threads,
Life's fondest moments, where laughter spreads.
Embracing our quirks, we look back and smile,
In the scrapbook of life, we dance all the while.

The Bridge of Understanding

We built a bridge with cookies and tea,
Negotiating with snacks, as happy as can be.
When words get tangled, and tempers can flare,
We throw in a pun, and it's laughter we share.

Through the clouds of confusion, we wave goodbye,
Making sense of madness, always willing to try.
With a dash of humor and a sprinkle of grace,
We find common ground in this funny old race.

Each miscommunication becomes a funny tale,
Like searching for the dog, only to find a snail.
Together we wander through life's little quirks,
In our bumpy ride, there's joy in the perks.

So let's keep connecting, with laughter in tow,
Building our bridge where the giggles can flow.
With a wink and a smile, we cross every stream,
Together in harmony, weaving our dream.

A Tapestry of Friendship

Threads of laughter weave through the night,
Braided with stories, oh what a sight!
Each stitch a memory, some silly and loud,
A tapestry vibrant, we wear it with pride.

From late-night talks to awkward first dates,
We share all the joys that patience creates.
In the fabric of life, our colors collide,
With a flicker of humor, we let love preside.

There's magic in mishaps, like spilled cups of tea,
We patch each mistake into comedy.
Our hearts all entwined, we dance and we weave,
Together we'll conquer, just watch us believe.

So here's to the laughter that binds us as friends,
In this joyful adventure, the fun never ends.
As we stitch our own quilt of the moments we share,
Let's keep laughing together, with love in the air!

Roots of Empathy

In the garden of my heart, a sprout we sow,
With laughter and giggles, we happily grow.
Sharing our snacks, and tales from the past,
Creating a bond that's designed to last.

A cactus with arms, oh what a sight,
Hugging the kites that take off in flight.
It's all about sharing, both giggles and cringe,
Even the grumpy can have a nice binge.

Eating spaghetti while riding a bike,
Try not to smile, it's a comedic hike.
With roots intertwined, and branches so wide,
We sway through this life, arms flung open wide.

So plant this garden, let kindness bloom,
With jokes and high fives that chase off gloom.
In the roots of our hearts, we'll discover a dance,
Where empathy flourishes, giving all a chance.

A Homage to Kindred Spirits

Two peas in a pod, or maybe more beans,
Navigating life with our froggy routines.
In pajamas we gather, while munching on fries,
Debating the merits of sushi and pies.

You snort when you laugh, and that's just fine,
Your humor runs deep like the best vintage wine.
With quirks and odd tales, we stroll hand in hand,
On this lighthearted journey, we form a grand band.

Underneath the stars, we dance without care,
Hopping like rabbits, in the cool evening air.
Each silly mishap becomes legend and lore,
Our kindred spirits, forever we'll adore.

Raise your glass of yogurt, we'll shout out with glee,
To friendships that flourish like a big leafy tree.
Here's to the laughter and love that we bring,
In this delightful world, we laugh and we sing.

Celebrating Diversity

From burgers to tacos, the world's quite a feast,\nEach
culture's a flavor, not new but not least.
Like gumdrops in sunshine, we sparkle and blend,
Creating a rainbow; let's share it, my friend.

In a hat made of fruit, I'll greet you with cheer,
With cupcakes of kindness, we'll banish all fear.
Dancing the tango with broccoli flair,
Expressions of joy float high in the air.

We're stirred, not shaken, in this funny mix,
An orchestra sounds, with the strangest tricks.
From bagpipes to banjos, let's strut and let's sway,
In this grand celebration, we've found our own way.

So gather your quirks, and let's take a stand,
For each wacky difference, together, we'll band.
With smiles like fireworks, we'll burst into light,
Diversity's a party; let's dance through the night.

The Poetic Pathway

On a pathway of giggles, with steps of delight,
We skip through our verses like bugs in the night.
With big clumsy shoes, we trip and we sway,
Every stumble a dance, in a whimsical way.

The rhymes are like bubbles, floating with glee,
As we sing silly songs beneath our own tree.
Each line a small treasure, wrapped up in a grin,
Where joy weaves together, and nonsense begins.

With scribbles and doodles, ahead we will roam,
Our footsteps lead back to the heart of our home.
In the scribbled pages of laughter and fun,
Our pathway connects us with everyone.

So grab your journal, let's write down our dreams,
With laughter as ink, we'll burst at the seams.
On this poetic journey, let's giggle and grow,
For life's a wild ride, come on, let's go!

The Dance of Acceptance

In a room full of awkward grace,
Everyone trips in a funny race.
With smiles so wide, we take the stage,
Embracing our quirks, like a sweet old page.

We spin and twirl with much delight,
Bumping into walls, causing a fright.
Laughter rings out, it's purely divine,
Even the chairs join in the line.

As we falter, we just play along,
Inventing new moves to our silly song.
Falling like stars, no need to pretend,
In this dance of ours, there's joy without end.

So let the rhythm guide your feet,
In this wacky world, there's nothing so sweet.
We'll clumsily sway to the beat of the day,
As laughter and friendship lead the way.

Graceful Steps Toward Peace

Tiptoeing softly on a bed of hope,
Stumbling awkwardly, oh how we cope!
With a wink and a nod, we shuffle around,
Our clumsy ballet is joyfully profound.

The music begins, and off we go,
Two left feet, oh what a show!
With every misstep, we cheekily grin,
In this dance of ours, we always win.

We slide and glide, avoiding the fight,
With handshakes and giggles, everything's alright.
Dancing our way through a colorful scene,
Together we conquer, know what I mean?

So here's to our steps, both graceful and odd,
Moving in rhythm with a bit of a nod.
Peace finds a way when we dance as one,
With each silly swing, the battle is won.

Colors of Connection

Painting the world in shades of delight,
With every stroke, we giggle with fright.
Our friendship a canvas, a spectrum so bright,
Mixing up colors in the warm, golden light.

We splash around hues of yellow and blue,
Creating a masterpiece—who knew?
With smudged hands and laughter, we truly connect,
Each silly blunder is perfectly decked.

A daub of pink here, a hint of green there,
Yelling "Oops!" as we splatter everywhere.
Like artists of joy, we bloom and grow,
In this colorful mess, our bond will show.

So let's mix our colors, with glee let's unite,
In this funny endeavor, everything feels right.
With brushes held high, let's create and refine,
A canvas of laughter, forever entwined.

Footprints of Forgiveness

In the sand, we leave quite the trail,
With goofy prints, we start to wail.
But the more we stumble, the more we learn,
Together we rise, in laughter we turn.

Each footprint a story, a tale to unfold,
Of mischief and mayhem, both gentle and bold.
With goofy mistakes, our hearts take flight,
Forgiveness is funny, in the warm sunlight.

We walk hand in hand, in our silly shoes,
Following echoes of laughter, our joyful muse.
Side by side, like two peas in a pod,
In our dance of amends, we'll give the world a nod.

So let's leave a trail, both silly and brave,
With footprints of joy, we happily pave.
In the sands of our journey, through giggles we drift,
Finding peace in our hearts is the ultimate gift.

The Sunlit Path to Reunion

We wandered off, a silly flight,
In search of snacks, not quite in sight.
Yet here we are, with smiles so wide,
Two goofballs laughing side by side.

The sun peeked out, a playful tease,
It whispered jokes, brought us to our knees.
We danced around, avoiding the ants,
With clumsy moves, we dared take a chance.

Our friendship's like a pizza pie,
Odd toppings mixed, but oh my, oh my!
With each bite, we share a laugh,
A recipe that's never half.

So let's skip rocks and laugh aloud,
Together, we're goofy and proud.
The sun will set, but not our fun,
In this silly dance, we both have won.

Weaving Common Threads

In a world of socks that rarely match,
We find the ones without a scratch.
With mismatched colors, we wear with flair,
Making fashion faux pas, but who cares?

Thread by thread, each laugh we weave,
In a tapestry of joy, we believe.
With witty quips, we stitch our fate,
Creating bonds that never abate.

Knots of laughter, tangles and glee,
We hold our seams with unity.
While others fret about frayed ends,
We focus on the joy that transcends.

So let's snap pictures, take a pose,
With silly smiles, laughter flows.
In this fabric, we find our way,
Friends forever, come what may.

A Sonata of Togetherness

Two kazoo players, off-beat and loud,
Create a symphony that draws a crowd.
With every honk, we shake and sway,
Making music in our own quirky way.

A xylophone made of pots and pans,
We strike a tune with clumsy hands.
Rhythms clash but hearts align,
This melody is truly divine.

The dance floor beckons, join the beat,
With silly steps, we can't be discreet.
Like two left feet in a right-footed world,
We spin and twirl, our joy unfurled.

Encore, encore! Our laughter rings,
Creating joy, oh, the joy it brings!
In this sonata, we are forever found,
In silly rhythm, we're joyously bound.

The Gentle Nudge to Forgive

You stole my fries, it's plain to see,
But here we are, just you and me.
With a wink and smile, let's start anew,
Those crispy bites, I'll share with you.

Mismatched socks can still bring cheer,
Like a friendly nudge when friends are near.
A giggle, a hug, can heal the sting,
Forgiveness blooms in the chirps of spring.

So let's trade stories, both silly and sweet,
Over a feast of our favorite treat.
With crumbs on our shirts and laughter at hand,
We stitch our hearts, together we stand.

In the end, it's love that prevails,
Even if a few faux pas derails.
So here's to us, let laughter reign,
With every giggle, we bless the pain.

A Mosaic of Gentle Words

In a garden where laughter blooms,
Petunias joke with the brooms.
Bees wear tiny goggles and buzz,
While daisies debate what was fuzz.

Squirrels argue about acorn wealth,
As dandelions achieve great stealth.
A sunflower reaches for the sun,
While tomatoes roll in a punny run.

Through the vines, whispers of cheer,
The thorns nod along, never fear.
A clover's luck brings a jest,
While mint throws 'em a zestful fest.

In this patch where humor grows,
Each leaf chuckles, the plant life knows.
A mosaic of quirky surprise,
Where even the shyest bloom tries to rise.

Unfurling Bonds

Two trees wave, their branches sway,
'You leaf me speechless,' they say.
Winds whisper secrets, all in fun,
As twinkling stars say, 'We've just begun!'

The daisies giggle, sharing delight,
Snails slide in with moves so slight.
Friendship grows in the garden's embrace,
As petals dance in a wobbly race.

A ladybug jokes about her flight,
'I've got spots, but they're all right!'
The sun grins down with a golden glow,
While shadows dance and put on a show.

In this realm where bonds unfold,
Each story shared, pure and bold.
Nature laughs, and so do we,
Creating bonds so carefree.

The Whispered Pact

Tiny ants huddle, form a pact,
'We'll carry crumbs, that's a fact!'
But one gets lost, things go awry,
    Ends up in a picnic pie.

Birds sit chatting on the wire,
'That worm was tasty, quite the fire!'
They laugh and squawk, share their finds,
In this world, no one's left behind.

A frog croaks jokes from the pond,
'The flies are quick, but I'm more fond!'
Water lilies roll their eyes with glee,
For every ribbit, there's more to see.

In whispered pacts, we all combine,
Where fun is woven, vine by vine.
Nature's humor, ever so bright,
A shared laugh, a true delight.

Starlit Alliances

High above, stars wink in glee,
'Look, a comet! Or just me?'
Galaxies giggle, spinning stories,
In the cosmos, all the glories.

Moonbeams stretch across the sky,
'Shining bright, but why oh why?'
The night laughs softly, a secret chat,
While shadows play beneath the mat.

Clouds trade jests, fluffy and light,
Catch a breeze, and take a flight.
Meteor showers bring dreams anew,
As laughter echoes, bright and true.

In starlit alliances, we find,
A universe filled, intertwined.
Where every twinkle shares a jest,
In this vast night, we are all blessed.

Nature's Gift of Amicable Ties

In a garden where daisies sway,
Bees dance round, in their own way.
A squirrel drops a nut in jest,
A bond that nature knows the best.

The sunbeams giggle on the trees,
While flowers gossip in the breeze.
A robin sings of friendship bright,
As critters plan a picnic night.

The ants march in a line so neat,
Carrying crumbs, oh, what a feat!
Together they share bites of cake,
Now that's a treat, make no mistake!

With every laugh, the petals bloom,
Creating joy in every room.
Nature's jesters, wild and free,
In every leaf, a jubilee.

Forging Bonds Among the Foliage

Underneath the leafy beams,
Squirrels plot their nutty schemes.
A rabbit joins with a cheeky grin,
'Let's race the wind, let the fun begin!'

The flowers sway, all colors blend,
Huddling close, they share, they spend.
Butterflies flutter, count to ten,
'We'll meet again, right here, amen!'

Grasshoppers leap with a boisterous cheer,
Discussing plans for a summer beer.
The daisies laugh at the clumsy flies,
And in their mirth, the whole world ties.

Nature's chuckles echo and roll,
Creating bonds that warm the soul.
In every corner, joy's alive,
Among the leaves, friendships thrive.

Gentle Hues of Togetherness

In the meadow where the laughter grows,
Kittens chase shadows, striking poses.
The lighthearted breeze gives a little poke,
And suddenly all the daisies choke.

A party of frogs croak a tune,
While the sun dips low, becoming a moon.
Fireflies twinkle, a lantern crew,
They say, 'Let's dance till we turn blue!'

Hummingbirds chirp their sweetest song,
Encouraging all, that's where they belong.
They sip from blooms, and wink their eyes,
In this camaraderie that never dies.

A tapestry spun with colors bright,
Whispering secrets under starlight.
Here in the wild, all are combined,
In gentle hues, together interlined.

The Language of Leaves

The leaves rustle, they start to chat,
'Is that a squirrel? Or just a hat?'
Branches tremble with giggles on high,
As birds practice jokes, to try and fly.

Grassy blades tap out a little song,
Singing along where all belong.
Mice share tales of their grand escape,
While turtles argue, 'We need a cape!'

Petals blush with each silly snort,
'Who'd have thought saplings could cavort?'
They scatter seeds of laughter wide,
In this woodland, no one must hide.

Nature's stage, a play of mirth,
Where animals unite, proving their worth.
Every leaf tells a tale of cheer,
In the language of nature, so sincere.

Ferns and Forks in the Path of Compromise

In a forest of ferns, we dance,
With forks in our hands, a ludicrous chance.
The squirrels giggle, they run and they tease,
While we argue over whose salad's a breeze.

Beneath leafy canopies, shadows do play,
Forks clinking together in a bright, silly way.
Who knew compromise could taste so absurd?
As wild veggies laugh, they sing just a word.

The dandelions wish they could join in the fun,
Poking their heads out, soaking up sun.
With each crunchy bite, the humor grows strong,
Nature's sweet chaos, where we all belong.

So here in the woods, let's settle the score,
With forks raised high, let's ask for some more.
In the laughter of leaves, find peace with a grin,
Ferns and forks gleam, let the friendship begin!

Songs of Friendship in Nature's Choir

In the heart of the woods, a choir takes flight,
Birds chirp out tunes, a whimsical sight.
Together we harmonize, a duet so sweet,
Yet one little frog just can't find the beat.

The bees buzz along, like they're part of the show,
While butterflies flit to and fro in a row.
We sing of our friendship, loud and off-key,
Joining in laughter, just you wait and see!

The trees start to sway, keeping time with our song,
A raccoon in the back seems to hum right along.
With each silly note, nature rolls with the smiles,
As we build our own memories, stretching for miles.

So gather your friends, let the giggles unfold,
In nature's own choir, your heart will feel bold.
From the laughter of branches, to songs sung so clear,
Friendship's sweet symphony is all that we hear!

The Gentle Exchange of Green

In gardens where greens meet, a chat takes place,
Lettuce and basil, no need for a race.
They trade funny tales of their growth in the sun,
While the tomatoes giggle, joining in the fun.

Cabbage rolls in, saying, "I'm quite the delight,"
"With layers to peel, I'm a sight for sore sight!"
The herbs laugh aloud, sharing stories of spice,
As carrots dig deep, rolling dice like mice.

With whispers of peas and the chatter of thyme,
Their exchanges of green turn harmony to rhyme.
Lettuce quips, "My leaves are crisp, cool, and nice!"
"No need for a dressing, I'm perfect in a slice!"

A feast on the table, laughter abounds,
In the gentle exchange, joy knows no bounds.
So next time you munch on your fresh, vibrant greens,
Remember their tales, their whimsical scenes!

Amidst the Leaves, Dreams Merge

Amidst swirling leaves, where whispers are spun,
Dreams merge together, oh what a fun run!
A squirrel chomps acorns, while birds share the news,
As wishes take flight, in colorful hues.

In the shade of the branches, we hatch silly schemes,
Creating a story from laughter and dreams.
A butterfly flutters, it joins in the play,
With wings that are dappled, a bright cabaret.

We toss leaves like confetti, let giggles take lead,
In the heart of the forest, there's no greater need.
For friendship's sweet laughter is our mingling glue,
As dreams greet each other, in skies ever blue.

So dance through the foliage, let worries take flight,
In the joyful chaos where dreams feel just right.
With each rustling leaf, may your spirit find cheer,
As amidst the great trees, we gather all near!

Dreams Merge

When night falls softly, and stars start to peek,
Dreams merge with laughter, they giggle and speak.
The moon winks down, a mischievous glow,
As shadows unite in a bright cosmic show.

In the fields where the daisies poke up from the ground,
Whispers of dreams echo all around.
A dandelion puffs out, the wishes take flight,
Carried by breezes that dance through the night.

With each gentle gust, the stories unwind,
In the glow of the stars, friendships are kind.
So gather your dreams, let them float on the breeze,
Amidst the chaos, the heart's thrill to seize.

As dawn draws near, with a stretch and a yawn,
The laughter of dreams paints the world like a dawn.
So hold onto the magic, embrace every part,
For dreams merge together, forever in the heart!

Beneath the Canopy

Underneath the leafy shade,
Squirrels dance in masquerade.
They chase each other round the tree,
While I sip my cup of tea.

Birds with tunes both sweet and wacky,
Create a symphony quite tacky.
A woodpecker, with such a knack,
Drills a message on my back.

A rabbit hops in perfect time,
As if participating in rhyme.
While bugs engage in aerial fights,
Complaining 'bout their awkward flights.

The breeze arrives, a gentle tease,
Whispers secrets through the leaves.
A party for the creatures there,
While I just laugh and take the air.

A Peaceful Heart

Supposed to meditate in peace,
But a fly just won't release.
It buzzes near my tranquil spot,
A tiny foe I have forgot.

I breathe in deep, try to relax,
But daydreams turn to silly acts.
Like racing squirrels in a duel,
While I become their laughing fool.

The trees around me seem to chat,
Discussing gossip, 'what's up with that?'
A squirrel with flair, a robin with style,
Makes this heartache worthwhile!

So I laugh, embrace the chaos neat,
As nature throws its wild retreat.
With giggles blended into the air,
I'm at peace—unless that fly comes back to stare.

Reverie in the Grove of Resolve

In the grove, I ponder life,
Swapped my troubles for some strife.
A raccoon grins with cheeky glee,
Daring me to chase it, whee!

A turtle joins, slow yet proud,
Irony wrapped in its shell, loud.
I swear it's plotting its own race,
While I'm just trying to find my place.

The breeze brings tales of wacky friends,
Whispering secrets with no end.
A stubborn breeze won't let me think,
Instead, it nudges me to blink.

So let's giggle at our grand parade,
With nature's laughter as our aid.
Lost in thoughts that feel absurd,
I'll take the wacky, not the weird.

Branches of Understanding

Branches stretch like silly arms,
Trying to catch the sun's charms.
A fruit hangs low, ripe for mischief,
Is it a snack or just a gift?

A clever crow caws overhead,
Declaring war on crumbs of bread.
While I debate if he's sincere,
He snatches a slice, 'thanks for the cheer!'

Nature's plushness well rehearsed,
A parade of chattering bursts.
Each critter talks in quirky tones,
I'm left giggling at their bones.

From laughter springs a hearty bond,
In the chaos, we respond.
Branches twirl in synchronized sway,
Cozy beneath the sun's ballet.

The Calm Between Storms

Before the rain, the world holds breath,
While frogs prepare a dance of death.
Splashing puddles, they croak with pride,
Chaos waits on the other side.

Clouds growl like they're telling jokes,
While lightning strikes at silly blokes.
What's better? To dance or hide?
The answer's clear: embrace the ride!

A snail takes a bow, slow and grand,
While raindrops plop on his one-man band.
'Tis the calm, a pause of fun,
Where each creature shines like the sun.

So here we are, let the storm pass,
As puddles form, we'll jump in mass.
Through ease and chaos, joy takes flight,
In every storm, find the delight.

Reaching for Unity

In a garden of jest, we plant our seeds,
With laughter as water, fulfilling our needs.
Witty weeds sprout, a bellyache brewing,
Yet together we laugh, our joy still ensuing.

A recipe crafted from quirks of our heart,
Mixing chaos and chuckles, a traditional art.
We juggle our hopes with a playful embrace,
In a world full of giggles, we find our own place.

A Glistening Token

A shiny small thing, forgotten in time,
It jingles and jangles, a ridiculous rhyme.
Made of old coins and a touch of false gold,
We clutch at this treasure, our fate to unfold.

Laugh lines are written in the creases of fate,
Each squabble a stitch in a great tapestry's rate.
We toss it in fountains with wishes for laughter,
And dance with our dreams, oh, what comes after!

Harmonious Embers

Our tales intertwine like vines on the wall,
With sparks of our humor igniting it all.
Each flicker of matchsticks, a comical fight,
We're kindling kindness, the glow is just right.

In this campfire circle, we roast all our gags,
While marshmallows melt, and our laughter just drags.
Let's toast to the wacky, the silly, the weird,
In the warmth of our fun, we are never feared.

Sweet Serendipity

Stumbling through life, we trip on our feet,
Accidental chuckles turn bland to sweet.
With socks that don't match and hair standing tall,
We toast to the blunders; they're the best of all.

Each slip is a lesson in giggles and grace,
In this odd little race, we find our own place.
Embrace the surprises, let laughter erupt,
For in the dance of chaos, we joyfully sup.

The Garden of Reconciliation

In the garden where we meet,
We plant laughter, oh so sweet.
Pickles grow on the apple tree,
And squirrels dance with glee, you see.

We water seeds of silly thoughts,
With jokes that tie our tangled knots.
A flower sprouts with a goofy grin,
As we chuckle, letting joy in.

Gnomes wear hats that spin and twirl,
They make the rabbits laugh and whirl.
Even bees buzz in a funny beat,
In this patch where love's a treat.

So let's dig deep, plant seeds of cheer,
Turn our frowns to silly gear.
In this garden, we find the way,
To bloom beneath the sun's bright ray.

Collages of Calm

In the gallery of wobbly frames,
We display our quirky, joyful games.
A painting made of mismatched socks,
Spawns giggles, echoes, and loud knocks.

A collage of puns and silly memes,
Where laughter flows like bubbling streams.
Each piece a moment, silly and bright,
Bringing calm with every slight.

We glue our quirks with glitter and glue,
Creating art that feels fresh and new.
A rainbow of laughter in every hue,
In this space, we let the fun accrue.

With crayons and doodles, we find our place,
A curious smile lights up each face.
Collages of calm, together we craft,
In our silly world, our spirits lift fast.

Tides Turning Toward Understanding

The tide rolls in with a wacky twist,
Silly boats bob, none can resist.
We ride the waves of laughter's call,
As understanding dances, big and small.

With surfboards made of foam and fun,
We paddle together, all as one.
Flip-flops fly like confetti in air,
Shower us with giggles everywhere.

The ocean tells jokes on salty breeze,
As jellyfish giggle with ease.
Understanding swells like the changing tide,
With humor as our goofy guide.

So let's splash in the waves of jest,
Learning together, feeling blessed.
In this sea of smiles, let's unite,
Turning tides like a kite in flight.

The Symphony of Togetherness

In the symphony of silly sound,
A tuba toots, and giggles abound.
The violin strings tickle the air,
As laughter fills the everywhere.

The drums beat out a funny tune,
And even the moon begins to croon.
With every note, we dance and sway,
Creating joy in a wacky way.

A harmony of hiccups and claps,
Melodies mix like friendly mishaps.
Together, we play this crazy score,
With silly solos that we all adore.

As the orchestra plays in delightful chaos,
We find the rhythm that brings us gloss.
In this cacophony, love takes flight,
A symphony of togetherness, so bright.

www.ingramcontent.com/pod-product-compliance
Lightning Source LLC
Chambersburg PA
CBHW051644160426
43209CB00004B/786